AL QAEDA'S NEW STRATEGY

Getting Back to Basics

A Novel by Rick D. Cleland

 www.trafford.com

North America & international
toll-free: 1 888 232 4444 (USA & Canada)
phone: 250 383 6864 ♦ fax: 812 355 4082

What is terrorism, fundamentally? It is to cause the general population to lose FAITH in the ABILITY of Government, at ANY level, to adequately protect the Citizenty. To create the belief or PERCEPTION among the GOVERNED, that individuals or Groups can act, at-will, in ways that threaten the daily safety of any or all citizens. Americans habitually over-react. Two airplanes, hijacked, crash into and destroy two buildings in New York City. A total of less than a dozen men are involved with four airplanes. Consequently, X-ray scanning machines are placed in almost all Airports and Checkpoints established (none "dubbed Charlie", thankfully). No longer can friends or relatives go directly to the gate for those departing or arriving. And the Terrorist haven't won for their cause? A Brit tries to set his shoe on fire ON AN AIRPLANE. The result is that all those going to board airplanes must remove their shoes. And the terrorists haven't won for their cause? Someone decides that innocuous bottles of liquid, when mixed in certain combinations, can become volatile and potentially explode. Therefore, a lady whose hair is dyed platinum blonde, has to leave her bottle of hydrogen peroxide in the trash can at the Entry Checkpoint. AND THE TERRORISTS HAVEN'T WON FOR THEIR CAUSE ?

Prologue

During the days of the Cold War with the former Soviet Union, American Embassies, Legations and Mission Buildings in Moscow, were built by State-owned Companies, using local labor and materials. That was a condition to be accepted in order to have a new Facility. It was well-known, and an accepted fact, that the building would be full of "bugs" and other "listening devices". Power and other Utilities supplied to the Building were under the control of local Government Authorities. Bills for such services were to be paid in USDs (US Dollars) and not Rubles, which were frequently 'devalued", by local Companies and Merchants. Consumer products used in food processing and preparation (flour, sugar, eggs and wheat), were available for commercial delivery on a very erratic schedule, since rail and trucking service was very undependable. One day a bakery might have 100 loaves of bread on hand and the next day, only 20 loaves. Meat delivery/availability was even more unpredictable. Little of it was taken from State-owned farms, since it was produced at State-subsidized prices - rubles - the value of which varied wildly, unpredictably, and fluctuated greatly. Most meat was bought from the Soviet Satellite "State" of Hungary, where beef, but more often, pork, and chicken were consistently plentiful and of excellent quality. The very existence of Hungary was, well, "tolerated" by the Soviets. They loathed and deplored it, for its fierce independence from the rest of Eastern Europe. Yet they admired the Magyar State for all of the same reasons.

When a completed American Government Building was turned over to the US Ambassador, the first Order of Business was to have the FBI scour it for listening devices. All phones were replaced with American-built-and -supplied new ones. Hung pictures were removed from walls and electronically-scanned for bugs. Live plants were routinely re-potted. Artificial, mostly silk plants, were checked with a "hand-held wand". Paneled and sheet-rocked walls were checked with a camera-like device that could detect changes in wall density - anything hung on the inside from the ceiling or attached to a stud - even rodents and their nests were detected. Everybody knew "the game" and how it was played. A device found was met with a shrug of the shoulder and a sheepish grin from the Construction Manager. His usual reply was a simple, "I didn't know that was there", in heavily-accented, but technically correct English. Then a terse "you idiot", in Russian to his underling standing nearby. Nobody bothered to check on the roof-top microwave transmitter and receiver, since all of those signals were 'encrypted' with computer-generated codes that changed too rapidly to be copied.

Typically, then, the Russian Construction Manager would have had the US Ambassador to sign the bottom of the Contract. The Building was, thus, accepted "as is" for the Government of the United States. The FBI would find the rest of the 'bugs" and remove them without mention. To have done otherwise, might have meant the "loss of face" to the Russians who were EXTREMELY SENSITIVE to that possibility. They'd rather lose a War than "lose face". The Ambassador would have extended his hand in "mock gratitude" to the Manager, who would have shaken it most vigorously. The Manager would then have grabbed both of the Ambassador's shoulders, pulling the two men together, as they touched cheeks - first one side and then the other, in the Eastern European tradition of mutual friendship. The big, ruddy-cheeked, heavy-set Russian Manager would then have exhorted, loudly, "da, eet ees done unt compleeted.. I sank you for your beeziness, kind Sir." Then, there would have been a symbolic handing of the keys to the huge, wooden front door, to the Ambassador with his Charge d'Affairs, and Commanding Officer of the Embassy's Marine Security Detail, standing just behind the Ambassador. The Russian Manager would then have then made a big, sweeping gesture with his right hand and arm, from the left side of his broad chest well-past his right shoulder. indicating that he and all of his men were vacating the property. AND THAT'S HOW IT WAS DONE during the days of the Cold War.

Al Qaeda "silent cell" Agent, Mohammed Mahmoud, knew THAT game well. He had studied it assiduously. He often reminded himself of the historian's cliche, "those who will not learn from History, are doomed to repeat it". For well over 200 years, the stupid Americans had REFUSED to learn even from their OWN history, much less that of Europe and Asia. The Great Wall of China was built to keep out the ravaging, rampaging Khubla Khan as his Mongols after they had cut a swath of death and destruction across Eastern Europe. It worked only partially, since there were never enough Chinese soldiers to police the Wall constantly. The Mongols simply threw up ladders and scrambled over the Wall. Erich Honecker, the nominal head of East Germany in Post WWII Europe, had built the Berlin Wall to keep the educated, Professionals (Doctors, Engineers, and Professors) from leaving the Communist bloc in East Berlin to avoid the Communist dogma and stagnant mindset. It had worked for a while with many would-be escapees being cut down in a hail of bullets fired from the automatic weapons of the dreaded Stasi (not-so-secret East Berlin Security Police). The Wall had worked for a while until the stubborn and independent-minded Hungarians finally provided some relief. They had simply opened a 100-foot gap in the chain-link and barbed-wife fence along their common border with Austria. East Germans would take a late-night train that passed that area of the border and pull the Emergency-Stop cord. When the train ground to a halt, the escaping Germans would bribe the train guards to open-fire, but deliberately fire high and over their heads while they ran across an open field and through the gap in the border fence to freedom in Austria. The Austrians would allow them safe passage to the West. And so it had gone for over 40 years until President Ronald Reagan paid a visit to just beyond the Brandenburg Gate and made his famous plea to the Soviets - "Mr. Gorbachev, tear down this Wall". It was roughly the same site where President John F. Kennedy had used a bullhorn to carry his voice over the Wall with HIS famous words of encouragement to East Berliners, "Ich bin ein Berliner" (I am a Berliner). Soon after Reagan's words to the Soviet Premier, Eric Honecker, terminally ill, had died. Erich Honecker, a Native East German, had been appointed by the Soviets to be the nominal President of East Germany. Mr. Gorbachev, whose wife, Raisa, was terminally ill, issued the Policy of "Glasnost" (openness, the forerunner to the more modern political term of TRANSPARENCY). Soon, long railroad trains of flat-bed cars, loaded Soviet tanks had taken them back, well inside what had been The Iron Curtain, another Political-term relic of the Soviet Union. The "Iron Curtain" was the name used to describe the many satellite Nation-States immediately bordering Russia. They all had "Puppet" Dictator-Presidents, firmly under the control of the Soviets, with the notable exception of Hungary, always the proverbial "independent and renegade" Nation. In the 1950s, the Soviets had tried to totally subjugate the Hungarians to the Soviet will. The Hungarians had rebelled. The brief and bloody rebellion was met with Soviet tanks, artillery and other heavy armor which had rolled through the streets of Budapest. The Hungarian resistance of mostly "Molotov Cocktails" was brief and showy, but proved no match for the Soviet tanks. The only purpose for the Iron Curtain was to provide a physical barrier for possible invasion from NATO and the West. Any Invader would have to first cross and conquer each one of them (Poland, East Germany, Hungary, Czechoslavakia, Yugoslavia, the Balkans, etc.) before stepping on Russian soil. That, theoretically, would buy the Russians the time needed to mount a vigorous defense and launch a counteroffensive. OR so the THEORY went. Another stupid Wall, thought Mohammed Mahmoud, to himself. Okay, two Walls that didn't work in the long term. Now, the Americans had learned nothing and were about to build yet another Wall. This time is was intended to keep Mexicans from illegally entering the US from the States bordering Mexico and attempt to discourage the illegal drug trade. Lots of money being spent to build a monstrousity of a concrete and chain-link Wall with the tacit message, "We dare you to cross it". What foolishness - what sheer stupidity. Didn't the Americans realize that building such an expensive Wall was tantamount to waving a red flag in front of a bull?

It was then that Mahmoud realized that the foolish Americans were about to play right into his hands. It was announced that Houston's Enron Building had been sold and at least one Bank would relocate there. Several foreign auto makers were interested in relocating their American Headquarters into the building. It was prime Houston real estate and offered close proximity to the Port of Houston which was the Port of Entry for cargo ships carrying autos from Japan and Korea. China was entering the international auto market and Houston was an attractive alternative port to Seattle, San Francisco, and Los Angeles. Its proximity, also, to the Gulf of Mexico and the Panama Canal were attractive to many Asian Pacific rim Nations. Even Vietnam and Taiwan, plus the Philippines, Malaysia, and Micronesia were considering industrializing into the international automobile market. Port Houston gave ready access to Southern Middle America via the North-South Interstate 35 , Texas-to- Minnesota, corridor, thanks to the North

American Free Trade Agreement. Mahmoud would not have to be inconvenienced by waiting for a new building to be constructed and having to somehow infiltrate the Trade Unions involved in the construction. Homeland Security was be forced to divert much of its human assets to oversee the construction of the Border Security Wall. That would force them to be less vigilant with the renovation of the Enron Building. A terrorist strike on the old Enron Building would carry the bonus of affecting the workers of international corporations and tie the hands of the State Department in responding to their concerns. It would be extremely disruptive - far beyond any actual damage to structure, human injury or actual loss of life. Now for the actual METHOD used for such a strike. No explosives of any kind would be necessary. Terrorism was not about causing damage to structures. It was about planting the seeds in individual's minds that Government, at ANY level, was incapable of adequately protecting its Citizens. As President Roosevelt, himself, had told the American people on December 8, 1941, after the Japanese attack on Pearl Harbor, "the only thing we have to fear is fear itself ...."

Mahmoud had his own plan. He would have to travel, now, to Central and South America, to make some contacts in order to provide himself and his Cause, Al Qaeda, with the necessary and critical supplies with which to carry out his Mission.

PARIS, FRANCE

Sitting in his friend's rented apartment, over a Bakery on a side street in Paris, Mohammed Mahmood, with a US Passport and a French Student Visa to take classes at the prestigious French Academie of Engineering, known, internationally, as the leading School for Aeronautical, Electrical, and Structural Engineering. Its graduates had designed the French high-speed monorail train system, components of the Mirage Military jet plane, and key parts of the Chunnel train. It connected England to France under the English Channel. He attended a few classes, but found the instruction to be geared largely to European-methodology Projects. He had really wanted to take Classes at Atlanta's Georgia Institute of Technology, but had no interest in the 100 and 200-level required Courses in order to take the 300 and 400-level Engineering studies. Georgia Tech had insisted on the entry-level classes. Mahmood had neither the time nor the interest in any of that. He did not want to attract the attention or suspicion of the Operative who took classes at the Florida Flight School in how to fly a 747 jet plane and then told the Instructor that he only wanted to fly it and not take it off or land it. He would get around that obstacle by using surrogates and paying them well for their time, talents, and expertise.

He was in a very pensive mood. He was Afghani-born, an Al Qaeda Member with Taliban sympathies. He was still in-Charge of the New York City Cell for Al Qaeda.. It was one of his men who conceived the idea of using "vibration-echo" to cause the Pan Am Building to collapse and then he quickly left New York and flew to Paris, using the circuitous route through Eastern Europe. Mahmood didn't see the need for all that travel - just additional expense, but his friend had insisted on it, to at least slow down the possible identification and pursuit by the Interpol

Police. Mahmood had finally acquiesced to it, to eliminate as much suspicion as was possible. The Chief Rizzo fellow of the New York Fire Department, had been very resourceful and may have finally put all of the pieces to THAT puzzle together. No way of knowing for certain, but Mohammed Mahmood felt himself to be safe and far enough insulated from his friend. He felt he should be able to remain uninvolved, and, more importantly, undetected and, therefore, uncompromised. THAT was the most important part - nobody knew or even suspected anybody besides the one who had tinkered with the Radio Station's transmitter.

Mahmood considered himself free to travel wherever, at will, and beyond suspicion. He could easily pass any and all Security checks at any Airport in the World, either entering or departing. His mind was the "dangerous weapon" - not anything he carried or possessed. He could easily be "profiled" by the stupid Americans, briefly detained and questioned, but his United States Passport should supercede all of that, hopefully. If interrogation were to continue beyond that, he would cite, that he should be no more suspect than American President Cameron, and the ACLU would gladly offer Lawyers to defend him at no cost to him. However, he had never had to resort to that and he did not anticipate having to do so in the near future. He would fly back to New York and assume his normal American identity as a good neighbor, taxpayer, and solid Citizen of the community. Even his wife had no clue as to his "outside" activities. He was a professional Consulting Engineer who traveled to where the work was. He enjoyed a decent salary, approaching six-figures. When home, he attended his young son's athletic events and his young daughter's school pep rallies, cheerleading, and dance recitals. He was an active member of the local Islamic Community, belonged to a Mosque, and even served, when he was home, as an Imam at the Mosque. "Outwardly" he was as 'normal' as any American walking the sidewalks and streets. That's the way Mohammed Mahmood wanted to seem to be - that's the way it had to be. His secret life as an Agent of Al Quada was a secret life that would follow him to his grave, unknown to even his wife and children. That's the way it had to be. For him, that's the only way it COULD be. Devise the Plan, hire or recruit the people to carry out the Plan, and then move on to the next Plan. It was all in the name of Islamic total World Domination. Total World allegiance to Allah - the Great One - and his will, to be carried out against the Infidels. Hitler and his Third Reich had fallen short and failed. Hitler had gotten his ego involved and moved too quickly into his Final Solution. Hitler might STILL have succeeded if he had not taken on the Russians when he did. He should have first eliminated the threat of Great Britain by continuing to support and fund Werner vonBraun's V-22 rocket program in the aerial siege of London. Had he continued to pound London, aerially, Prime Minister Winston Churchill would never have been able to rally the 'British spirit' with his "this has been our finest hour" speech. He could have ignored and temporarily by-passed the Russians and the entire Eastern Front. Hitler's timing had been terrible. By postponing his invasion of Russia until the Spring of 1944, he would not have had to deal with the severe Winters of Leningrad/ Saint Petersburg. That is where Adolph Hitler, the Fuhrer, had made his fatal mistake. Al Qaeda and Leader Osama bin Laden would not fall into that trap and make the same mistake. Al Qaeda would be more patient and careful. Al Qaeda had time on its side, as did Ho Chi Minh and the North Vietnamese. Americans are impatient and impetuous. They wanted "instant success, and financial reward and instant gratification". Asians do not fall into that trap. They will "wear down" the American will to continue the fight and prevail over the months and years. Americans have "no stomach" for waiting for success over the long term. Mahmood would now move back to New York City. Al Qaeda had already accomplished its goal there - terrorism. It had destroyed two important symbols of both Commerce and Engineering with the Twin Towers of the World Trade Center and the PanAm Building. One had been very messy and one had been rather "artful". One had used brute force, with fire, flame, and intense heat. The other had used "finesse" and technology. One had caused human death and suffering. The other had not taken a single life, but many with injuries. The Modus Operandi had been the same and had been Al Qaeda's "signature" - terror, as in FEAR. President Roosevelt had aptly defined it on December 8th, 1941, when the Japanese had attacked Pearl Harbor and he had issued a Declaration of War against the Japanese Empire. He spoke to the American people, those infamous words, "the only thing we have to fear is fear itself. Nameless, faceless, unjustifiable FEAR". The fear of leaving one's house, of turning the key in the ignition of one's car. The fear of simply opening the garage door - you would not KNOW what was on the other side of the door until you actually opened it. The fear of simply leaving the warmth and comfort of your bed on a cold, Winter morning. Did the furnace provide heat throughout the night? Had the water heater worked to provide you with hot water for a shower in the morning? Would the valve work to mix hot and cold water to provide tepid water to wet your hair, shampoo it, and rinse off the shampoo? Would anyone have tampered with the toothpaste, at the store, to damage your teeth. Would anyone have opened your multi-vitamin capsules and added some kind of poison - maybe a neighbor, friend, or guest at last night's party?

That was the "definition" of terror - to get you to question everyone any everything. To cause you to live in constant fear and to question absolutely EVERYTHING in your daily interaction with everyone with whom you might come in contact. To get you to voluntarily withdraw and live in isolation. THAT was the aim and the goal of those engaged in terrorism.

Al Qaeda had decided to SHIFT its Operations somewhat. The US Department of Homeland Security had heavily concentrated its manpower (a very heavy expense) on New York City and the many miles of border that the US shared with Mexico. It was erecting a "Berlin-style" concrete Wall along hundreds of miles of its Southern Border to do two things, principally. First, stem the tide of illegal immigrants. Second, reduce (outright elimination was a mere 'pipe dream') the flow of drug traffic into the US from the Mexican Drug Cartels. The hope was that in the process of doing so, they might also catch an occasional Al Qaeda Agent. That would be an exercise in frustration, since the only "crime" would be to have improper documents in their possession. Upon being "caught", the ILLEGAL would be jailed and then appear before a local Magistrate with an INS Agent present. The illegal would be Ordered deported immediately. It was tantamount to trying to sneak into a bar among a crowd, He'd get stopped, his ID summarily declared fake, and get kicked out. He'd walk to a less heavily-trafficked door, slip the Bouncer a 'twenty', whereupon the Bouncer would turn his head to one side to fake a sneeze, and the Illegal would "waltz right in". However, instead of a bar and a twenty, the Illegal would try at the next Border town and 'up the ante' of the bribe to a C-Note or more, as necessary. It was not at all hard to do, it just took time, patience, and determination (plus the everpresent wad of twenties, fifties, and Hundreds in one's pocket). Being glib would no longer suffice. It boiled down to the old cliche of "money talks and bullshit walks".

On the trans-Atlantic Air France flight from Paris' Orly, to New York's JFK, Mohammed had plenty of time to both rest and think. "What's my next move and where?" He recalled the cinema of "The Towering Inferno", wherein a tall building caught fire due to sub-standard wiring performed by a Contractor who used insulation that was "not up to Code", in order for his bid to be just below the Project Budget for the Electrical portion of total construction cost. The "EE" had bid, citing the use of the Code-correct wiring, but at a much less costly price. The Project Manager had approved the bid and accepted it, knowing full-well that the Code-correct wiring could not be purchased at the price quoted in the bid .He also knew that the wiring described in the bid was of much higher "insulation-quality" than the wiring that would actually be installed. The cost in savings, under the Electrical Budget, was "kicked-back" to the Project Manager. Nobody knew anything different, until there was a Circuit overload in a large refrigeration Unit that caused two 220-Volt wires to overheat. The wires were almost touching, inside a junction box near the top of the high-rise Building. One wire "arced" to the other, easily burning through the cheaper insulation, and setting fire to the entire junction box. The intense heat quickly melted the rubber grommets where the wires entered through 'punched-out' metal holes of the junction box. With the rubber grommets gone, the heat had a source of oxygen. Flames quickly shot out of those holes and ignited nearby combustible materials. The building was now on fire and well-beyond the capability of any hand-held fire extinguishers. Fire alarms were pulled and fire hoses jerked from their glassed-in wall boxes. People waited for the heavy, bulky, flattened fire hoses which they held, to fill with water. The valve for the water was inside the case where the hose had come from. Nobody thought about that. As the heat from the fire grew more intense, those holding the still-flattened fire hose gave up and just dropped them.

Could Al Qaeda arrange for another "towering inferno"? Not EXACTLY, BUT there was another alternative. What about tinkering with a building as it was ACTUALLY BEING CONSTRUCTED? Was there a likely City where that might occur in the near future? Chicago? Los Angeles? San Francisco? Denver? Atlanta? Miami? Dallas? Houston? He eliminated all but three Cities as "possibles" - Chicago, Dallas, Houston. He knew of no new, large buildings scheduled for construction in Chicago, but the area was "ripe" - the upper midwest. Dallas and Houston were next. Both Cities in Texas with its grandiose "reputation" and bordering on Mexico. Nothing big planned there, somewhat still reeling from the problems incurred from Hurricane Katrina. Dallas, on the other hand, had a hotel and Convention Center scheduled for construction. In fact, its Mayor had campaigned quite heavily for it and narrowly got City funding for it, courtesy of the Taxpayers. It had been a very divisive and contentious issue in the recent election. A lot of the Contractors whose bids had been accepted, were going to have to hire skilled labor from the local market. The REALLY skilled labor was already tied up with other area construction. That would leave the marginally skilled labor of the Hispanics in this Country on temporary Visas as Seasonal workers and Day Laborers - the so-called "Green Card" holders. Dallas, as a site, had definite possibilities but Mohammed Decided that it would take too long for a plan to develop. Also, to be considered, was that Dallas had a reputation for a very fickle City Council. It was often difficult to get a majority vote, particularly on large capital expenses. To please one Group was to automatically alienate another Group. A Convention target was a very tempting target, since Events held there would attract large gatherings of the general public. However, the City Manager would be monitoring

Minority Contractors very closely for compliance with Federal and State labor laws. The risk of a violation in that area would result in a Lawsuit and a possible Restraining Order temporarily stopping construction. There was also the matter of considerable Taxpayer funding for the Project. It had very narrowly passed even when strongly supported by the Mayor. The next election might result in a Taxpayer Revolt and a roll-back of the City taxes needed to complete the Project. Too "iffy" - too many potential problems for Mohammed. Houston was looking better and better for the next "strike" by Al Qaeda. Mohammed would make no final decision yet, but he was close to one and he had the authority to make the final decision of where to attack next.

DEALING WITH DRUG KINGPINS

Mohammed Mahmoud took a flight out of New York's JFK Airport for Cancun, Mexico. It suited his "front" perfectly as a man of obvious Middle Eastern origin on vacation in sunny Cancun, directly on the Gulf of Mexico. Mexican Customs Officials looked at his Passport and noted that it showed dual-Citizenship - American and British. This raised no particular concern, since both Countries had large numbers of Native Middle Easterners among their multi-Cultural populations. He said that he was on business as a Representative of an American Distilled Spirits Distributor to consummate new Contracts with individual growers of the Agave plants which produced Tequila for the International Market. Without being asked, he produced documents proving his entitlement to import Distilled Spirits from Mexico, directly into the United States. He was asked if he was carrying more than Ten thousand American Dollars in Cash, on his person. He replied that he was NOT and did not mind a "pat-down" to prove it. He was aware of the Mexican Law that required a Cash Amount of over Ten Thousand American Dollars, carried on one's person, to cause an automatic Delay of Entry for two business days, while Authorities determined that it was not intended for the purchase of illegal drugs. He carried only Certified Banque Checques with the Payee Line already filled in. Did they want to see them? No, they did not. Mohammed caught a break since he was bluffing. The Checks were made out to Cash. He cleared Mexican Customs and caught a cab to his hotel. He checked in at the Front Desk, gave his American Express Card Number, got his room key, picked up his one suitcase and went straight to his room. He made a few telephone contacts and returned to the Lobby where he was sitting in the hotel lounge, when he noticed a group of American adults arriving in Taxis at the front door of the Hotel. That caught his attention as somewhat odd, since it was normally around this time of the Spring when College Students flooded Caribbean and Mexican resorts on their Spring breaks. Young people were a common sight, but adults were something of a rarity. He made a few discreet inquires of the Concierge and found that is was a Wedding Party arriving from Houston. The bride and groom were both Lawyers with different Law Firms in Houston. He was with a Firm which had just leased several floors in the soon-to-be-renovated former Enron Building. "Wow, what luck", thought Mohammed, silently, to himself. Two Lawyers and one of them with a firm about to move into the very building he was going to set up for a terrorist attack. The Desk Manager quickly reminded the Concierge that his Duty was to assist guests with information about Cancun, where to go and how to get around. It was none of his business who the guests were, where they had come from, what they were doing in Cancun or Mexico, or why they were staying at this particular Hotel.

Mohammed quickly did his "homework". He found out the names of the Bride and Groom and where Wedding flowers and Gifts were to be displayed. He arranged for a modest floral display to be in the appropriate area. He also arranged for one complete place-setting of the chosen dinner China to be placed on the Gifts-table. The card was signed, "I am pleased to make your acquaintance. I am from Houston, here on business. I wish you both a life of happiness and bliss, together. Most Sincerely, Mr. Mohammed Mahmoud".

At the reception, Mohammed properly identified himself to the bride and groom and all of the members of the Wedding Party. He enjoyed just one glass of fine, imported French Champagne, and then retired to his room for the rest of the evening. He would retire slightly early, get a good night's rest, and make his business contacts in the morning. He had recently "groomed" himself to look "ready" to deal with Native Mexicans. He stood at 5'10" and 200 pounds. His thick black hair was combed straight back with a slight uplift at the nape of his neck. He wore a short black beard with a "pencil-thin" black moustache. He wore a straw Panama hat and carried an internationally-licensed 9 millimeter pistol on his belt at the rear of his waist, under the jacket of his Palm Beach suit. He had earned a black belt in jujuitsu and could use karate quite effectively. His hands were large and strong and his fists carried a lethal punch, thrown straight from his strong shoulders. If necessary, he'd throw a punch straight at his opponent's nose, driving it back into his brain - death was almost instant. He had never had to use his expertise in the Martial Arts, but these Mexicans had a reputation of not exactly "playing fair" and he was taking no chances. His own 9 millimeter was no match against an Israeli Uzi with a fifty-round clip. After several calls, he finally got in contact with Senor Pedro Fuentes who owned a 500 acre Agave cactus farm. Mohammed wanted to buy enough agave leaves to make 500 cases of Tequila. They would be placed in metal containers, export taxes paid to Pedro's AMIGO ENTERPRISES, and shipped to "Consignee", Port of Houston, Texas. The numbers of Mohammed's Export/ Import License, typed on the Bill of Lading, would match those on the Identification Papers presented to Port of Houston Authorities, by Mahmoud's man as representing the Consignee. The metal boxes of agave cactus leaves would be trucked to a legitimate Distiller of Tequila in New Mexico to enhance Mahmoud's cover. Somewhere, en route, the delivery truck would make a stop where the metal boxes would be opened and the leaves gently probed with thickly-gloved hands. The hands would gingerly search through the leaves until an estimated 50 scorpions and/or tarantula spiders were found and moved to a glass aquarium-terrarium, and warehoused for safekeeping until Mahmoud had further use for them. So far, Mahmoud's plan was evolving quite nicely. However, it was FAR from over.

Mohammed's next trip was a short flight to Managua, Nicaragua. His contact was a Senor Pablo Valdez, the Owner of a large banana Plantation. Mohammed had absolutely no interest in trafficking in drugs, the venture for which Kingpins Fuentes and Valdez were best known. His interests were solely in the legitimate businesses in which both men engaged as a FRONT for the much more lucrative "crops" of both cocaine and marijuana, but principally, cocaine. Mohammed was only interested in buying agave cactus leaves to be distilled into tequila, and bananas which had a wide variety of uses in the American consumer market. More than once, both Fuentes and Valdez had offered Mohammed an opportunity to deal in drugs. He had been sorely tempted, but fat profits were not his motivation - furthering the Cause of Al Qaeda was his prime and only concern. Those who dealt in drugs had to constantly watch their backs for Agents, informants, and their paid surrogates.

He well remembered what happened to John Z. DeLorean , who had been a Senior Vice President of Ford Motor Company. After the fiasco of the Edsel, DeLorean had proposed his own cencept of an automobile. It was a good concept, but it was a classic case of "the Message being ignored for dislike of the Messenger". John DeLorean had resigned from Ford and founded DeLorean Motor Company in order to produce his car. Ford's Chairman called all of the banks usually used to finance the Auto Industry and "pressured" them to deny any start-up loans to John DeLorean. Faced with having been cut-off for START-UP cash at the Banks, DeLorean had turned to the only source left to him. He "went South" of the border to Mexico and found the cash he needed from one or more of the Drug Cartels. Soon, DeLorean automobiles, made in Mexico, began showing up in American Showrooms of both Ford and General Motors Franchisees. General Motors was large enough that it just "blinked" at the competitor, kind of like a pesky mosquito refusing to be shooed away from the end of one's nose. It was a nuisance - an annoyance, but no real threat YET. However, a little known fact to the average automobile owner (warrantees notwithstanding), is that when something goes wrong with their car, more often than not, a part has malfunctioned and needs to be replaced. Duh, no surprise there, right? Of course. That means that a complete inventory of replacement parts must be either in-stock at the Dealership, or readily available on short notice. THAT'S what caused the demise of John Z. DeLorean and his fledgling Automobile Company. Roughly speaking, for every dollar he had invested in the manufacture in one of his cars, he needed five dollars to invest in replacement parts. NOW, he needed Big Bucks - large amounts of CASH ON HAND to pay American suppliers. He could ill-afford to have one of his cars occupying a bay at a Dealership's Service Shop, waiting on a replacement part sitting on a shelf of a part's Supplier Warehouse for delivery, for lack of payment for the part. Soooo, John DeLorean had turned, in his desperation, to the Mexican Drug Kingpins of Cartels, for fast cash. None of THEM "ratted" on John DeLorean. The arrangement suited them just fine. Ford Motor Company knew exactly where to look. Spare parts are a very heavy "up front" expense. They had arranged for all of the Banks to cut-off DeLorean Motors for credit. That left only two possible and plausible sources of large sums of money quickly and potentially untraceable, remaining. Either DeLorean had a lot of wealthy SILENT PARTNERS underwriting his venture,

OR, there was Drug Money involved. Ford took a reasonable gamble and guessed it was the latter. They placed ANONYMOUS TIPS to Treasury, INS, ATF, and the FBI. John DeLorean was caught, tried, found guilty of receiving money illegally, and sent to Federal Prison. His Company went Bankrupt. AND THAT was the lesson that Mohammed had learned the EASY way, in not to deal with Drug Dealers in order to achieve his goals and succeed in reaching his Objectives for Allah and the Al Quada. Now to meet with Pablo and buy his bananas.

Mohammed had worked, as a teenager, in a Grocery Store near his home. Grocery Stores typically put such "temporary or Summer" hirees in the Produce Department. They do so because that is where a lot of spoilage is expected to occur. The produce Department of any large grocery Chain is known as "the loss leader". It is where "profit" never occurs and it exists solely for the convenience of customers. Most everything is sold by-the-pound and weighed on scales located in the Produce Department. At the time, the scales had a piece of curved glass covering the weight-readout. If you were about 5" 7" and looked through the glass "dead-on", you got an accurate weight-reading". Not so, if you were five feet-five inches tall (or shorter) , as are most women who, at that time, did most of the grocery shopping. The most expensive Produce item at that time were the stemmed ,seeded, red cherries, at about 69 cents a pound. That made one cherry in a small clump, cost about a nickel. At that time, a nickel was roughly equivalent to a quarter today. By the time that young Mohammed peeled off all of the dead or unsightly leaves from the heads of lettuce and cabbage, what remained was about the size of an average grapefruit. Part of his job was to go to the back of the store where EMPLOYEES ONLY were permitted and open the heavy cardboard crates that contained the bananas which had been delivered just before sunrise and shoved down a metal chute with steel rollers on ball bearings used the force of gravity to take the boxes and crates through small openings into the Store's Stockroom. All other grocery items were delivered during daylight hours. Cases of beer and cigarettes were sent down the same metal chute, but were diverted through a smaller opening, into a steel-wired cage for a "Receiving Inventory" count, by the Store Manager, which, hopefully, MATCHED the Delivered Inventory count. Any discrepancies had to be resolved IMMEDIATELY, since all alcohol and tobacco Products were taxable by the Selling Entity immediately upon receipt without regard as to whether they were eventually purchased by customers. For the young Mohammed, it was the boxes of bananas that were the most interesting. His boss, Angelo, told him to open the heavy cardboard boxes and remove the "hands" of bananas. He was to place them on a metal cart and push them out the hinged double doors and place them "attractively" on a slightly slanted wooden display stand. However, he was warned by Angelo, to be careful as he removed each hand of bananas from the box. Sometimes, there were tarantula spiders hidden among the bananas. To avoid them, it was best to pick up each hand of bananas and shake it vigorously to dislodge any "unwanted visitors".

Mohammed never forgot that advice and experience. Now he was on a mission in Nicaragua to actually buy bananas as an Agent for banana Sellers in the United States. He didn't give a damned about the bananas - it was those "hitchhiking" tarantula spiders that he wanted to be hidden in the boxes of bananas he was going to arrange to have exported into the United States. He would pay Pablo Valdez One Hundred US Dollars for every tarantula he could arrange for his pickers to slip into the boxes among the bananas - a minimum of 100 tatantulas. Pablo Valdez expressed curiosity as to the sudden interest in such spiders in the US? Mohammed had anticipated the question and had a ready answer. He told Valdez that some kind of a small worm was boring its way into the tall and picturesque Suguaro Cactus, native to New Mexico and Arizona and causing devastation to the plants. Tarantula spiders were the only known creatures that could kill these worms by sucking the juices out of them. The juices in the worms were highly toxic to all but the large and hairy tarantula. The explanation made sense to Pablo who was really only interested in the 100 USDs cash for each spider. He DID ask if such an order would be ongoing or just a one-time deal. Mohammed's answer was that he would have to wait and see how effective the spiders were in controlling the invasion of the worms. As far as passing US Customs, Mohammed was not overly concerned. Agricultural US Customs might notice a few of them lying on top of the bananas, but would never suspect that there were many more deliberately placed there. Even those who noticed a critter or two would probably not be bothered, since there was no incentive to do so. They were not narcotics, after all, and they had no significant "street value" or demand inside the US. They would be sent to the same ultimate delivery address as the scorpions hidden among the cactus leaves and handled in the same way until Mohammed or one of his men had further use for them.

Mohammed Mahmoud had finished his business in Mexico and Nicaragua. He checked out of his hotel without incident and took a cab to the Airport in Managua for his direct flight to Houston where he had much work to do in preparation for the occupancy of the renovated Enron Building, for which a new name had not yet been chosen.

The Two Phases

Phase One was for Mohammed to "blend in" as best he could with the other tenants of the renovated building, which was renamed "RONNE Tower" (pronounced "Ronnie" as a cost- saving measure in signage, since it utilized all of the letters of the old Enron Building with the letters simply rearranged). Mohammed would maintain a "neighborly" image with his frequent comings and goings. His Importing Business was quite legitimate, supplying Central and South American bananas and fruits (avocados, macadamia and pistachio nuts)to grocery retailers, and agave cactus leaves to American Distillers in the Southwest. He was fully Licensed and properly, legally incorporated as an LLC. He could easily pass any document check that the State of Texas or the Federal Government might perform on him or his Entity/Enterprise. He made a habit of stopping each morning at a nearby Starbucks Coffee Shop and chatting with the other customers. It killed him to pay their inflated prices for coffee with so much added to it that the taste of coffee was barely discernable. However, to his neighbors in the Ronne Towers and some other nearby buildings, it was like being hooked to an oxygen tank with two small, plastic prongs inserted into their nostrils. They were "hooked" and they were dependent and in desperate of their morning "fix". Some stared, blankly, into their laptop computer screens with the little plug-in computer memory chip that connected them to the coffee shop's Wi-Fi system. None appeared to be following the Stock Market. All seemed to be reading their E-Mail and responding to it. As far as he could determine, they were doing nothing that could not have waited until they were at the desk in their Office(s). Apparently there a need to impress those around them with their "tech savvy-ness". They were all dressed appropriately professionally, except for one particular detail. None were wearing conventional, leather shoes. To a person, they were all wearing some kind of athletic shoe with more rubber under their feet than was probably on the tires on their cars. A few ladies wore boots with spike heels. The leather went all the way up to their knees. Ah, well, such is life, thought Mohammed to himself. He had to get back to his Office to check on the status of his various shipments from Mexico, Central and South America. The agave cactus leaves concerned him the most, since most Tequila entered the United States already distilled into the final product and bottled. To the average American consumer of distilled spirits, it was little-known that most off-brand-name Gin, Vodka, and Tequila, was imported by ocean-going tankers and then pumped into railway tank cars. These were taken to railroad sidings to such as the giant Seagrams Distillery in northern New Jersey. Tequila was similarly imported, mostly through the Port Of Houston. Large hoses were attached to nozzles on the tanker cars and the almost pure grain alcohol was sucked into huge tanks at the site of the "distillery". It is THERE that the ingredients for the actual formulas to give the distinctive "tastes" to the final product was added and then "bottled". BRAND names of distilled spirits do not go through this process.

Such as Beefeater or Tanqueray or Boodles Gin are actually imported already bottled. The higher price you pay for those products, reflects that fact. Almost all Scotches also fall into this category - they are distilled in Scotland, actually bottled there and sent, by cardboard or wooden caseload, via ocean-going ship, to their Port-of-entry into the United States - usually New York or New Jersey. Almost all Whiskey and Bourbon is actually distilled and bottled in the States of Kentucky or Tennessee. What is known as "blended Whiskey" is distilled mostly in Canada. Vodka is quite another story. It is distilled from the fermentation of common, garden-variety potatoes. It is distilled mostly in eastern Europe and Russia. It is somewhat a "staple of life" there, much as iced-tea is a staple of life in the South of the United States, and wine is a staple of life in France, Italy, and Greece. Vodka is typically at least 40% grain alcohol. Those who consume it regularly gain a certain "tolerance" to it which means that they are in a perpetual sort of "low-grade drunk" . Since nobody has ever seen them in any other state, THEIR "drunkeness" becomes their normal state. The best example of this is the former Chairman of the Soviet Communist Party, Nikita Khrushchev. He was always so "drunk" on vodka, that it became his "normal" , albeit, crude and obnoxious, behavior. This "state" eventually caused his eviction from the Politburo of the Supreme Soviet and his "retirement-in-disgrace". He was afraid of flying in airplanes, and so when he came to New York City in the early 1960s to address the General Assembly of the United Nations, he actually crossed the North Sea and Atlantic Ocean from Vladivostock, in extreme North Russia, as a passenger on a "tramp freighter". He landed at Boston harbor and took a helicopter (apparently he could tolerate flying as long as it was slow and he could see the Earth below) to JFK Airport and landed in a remote area of the airport. He was driven, by car, to a waiting jetliner and entered by a rear door. He then simply walked the length of the inside of the jet to the front door and "appeared to have arrived by jetliner". He then appeared before the General Assembly of the United Nations and gave his infamous speech wherein he took off his shoe, banged it on the podium and summarily declared to the United States, "we will bury you". He then departed by helicopter to Boston where he again boarded a "tramp freighter/common cargo ship" back to Vladivostock. He could not travel without being drunk on vodka. On the voyage back to Russia, he was seen by several members of the crew, leaning over the top rail and vomiting into the ocean below. Mohammed clearly remembered THAT incident. He was, therefore, HOPING that his raw agave cactus leaves would not raise undue suspicion with the Border Patrol, INS, or Homeland Security. He had a plausibly answer, but he hoped the shipment would not raise a suspicion that would require an explanation. He had a bit of a scare when he got word on his cell phone that the vans carrying his cactus leaves were stopped at the Texas-New Mexico border. They were suspected of carrying illegal alien migratory farm laborers. Seeing no human cargo, the Officers suspected illegal drugs and opened several of the many wooden cases. A single scorpion crawled out of one of the opened cases and got on the Officer's hand. Recognizing what it was, the Officer quickly shook his hand and the scorpion fell onto the floor of the van where he squashed it with the sole of his shoe. He yelled to his colleagues, "holy shit, these cases of leaves are infested with insects from Mexico. I ain't paid to deal with anything alive unless it's human. Gimmee a hammer to nail them shut again and fuck this damned shit. We're outta here. Tell the drivers to shut their rear doors and drive these vans the hell outta Texas. Fuck, let the Feds or the New Mexico Police deal with this crap." And so, a potential problem had been averted. The vans arrived at a metal warehouse in southern New Mexico and drove up a concrete ramp into the warehouse where they were expected. The door to the warehouse was quickly closed and a dozen men, paid $100 cash, each, for their time and labor, began unloading the 100 wooden "beer-case-sized" crates from the vans. An ingenious device had been rigged-up to quickly separate the scorpions from the agave leaves. It was a very large metal funnel about six feet across at the top, tapering down to a hole about the size of a basketball. One-by-one, each of the 100 crates was opened with a man on each side, and quickly flipped upside down and tapped against the side of the funnel to dislodge its entire contents. A device was rigged to the funnel, much like the device used in retail paint stores to mix and stir-up cans of paint. It vibrated the entire metal funnel to separate the scorpions from the agave leaves. The tarantulas all fell through the hole at the bottom of the funnel and dropped directly into a metal box filled with excelsior and perforated on top with holes that could have been made with a common ice-pick. There WAS one little surprise that was easily handled. The Mexican agave farmer had apparently tossed-in, free, a couple of diamondback rattlesnakes. They were quickly killed by the workers - they'd got hung-up in the hole at the bottom of the funnel, trying to wriggle back up the slick sides of the metal funnel. As they eventually slid, head-first, through the hole, they were decapitated by the workers with, (what else), trusty box-cutting razor knives. They would be skinned and cut-up into small chunks for a tasty meal. In the Southwest, rattlesnake meat was a delicacy and tasted somewhat like chicken. The funnel could process about 6 cases at a time. Then, the funnel was moved about ten feet by cables attached to a track in the ceiling. The hinged bottom was opened and all of the agave leaves fell out into a large, heavy cardboard box. And so it went, six cases at a time, until all 100 cases were emptied. The entire process took about an hour and that's all the time they had until others who had rented space in the warehouse would begin arriving for pick-ups or deliveries. The first part of Phase One had been successfully completed without creating any suspicion. OR HAD IT ? Was Mohammed becoming paranoid, or had he REALLY pulled it off ? The incident with the vans being stopped bothered him. Had the Officers been "tipped off" or were they really looking for just "illegals" and drugs ? If they WERE looking for a shipment of scorpions, they HAD found them, and wouldn't have given a damned about the cactus leaves. Another thing bothered him. None of the Officers had asked what all of those cactus leaves were to be used for. He had a plausible reason, including a false Bill of Lading from a fictitious distiller, who had placed the Order, marked "Paid-in-full", but with no Invoice Amount listed. Had his vans been followed? If so, it wasn't by any marked Police or Patrol car. The van drivers had hand-held Police scanners and would surely have heard something. Crossing State lines would have required a Unit of some Federal Agency. No kidnappings had been reported by a Nation-wide "Amber-Alert", so the Federal Mann Act did not apply. He decided to ask around the warehouse about any unusual or suspicious vehicles having been in the area. No, nothing out of the ordinary. He decided to put his suspicions and fears to rest and concentrate on the second part of Phase One, Part 2 - the bananas with the tarantulas. Phase One, Part 3, the fleas and ticks could wait.

Bananas were much easier to deal with. They were a high-demand commodity in the US. Just to mention one, how long would Gerber Baby Foods survive without a constant supply of bananas? A couple of tarantula spiders in any shipment were almost expected. They were almost welcomed. They fed on the many insects that tried to bore small holes in the banana peels to get to the soft, sweet fruit inside. Absent tarantulas and there was no natural predator for whatever might be trying to penetrate the banana. The wholesale cost to the retailer for bananas was not a great concern. In grocery stores, bananas were considered a "loss leader". With the spoilage rate of bananas being so high if not purchased with a day or two of display, they were heavily "discounted" to be sold quickly. Brown or browning bananas had a market limited to those who wanted them for immediate use in baking recipes. The loss on the sale of bananas would be made up by the profit made by items in the canned or boxed food sections of the store. Meat and Seafood Departments of a retail store stood on their own merits as far as profit to the store is concerned. They are an Entity unto themselves, and because of their need for constant refrigeration (especially pork, chicken, and fish), they are always priced "highly competitively" with every attempt made to sell them in bulk (hence the terms, "value pack" and "family pack"). Unknown to the general public, crates of bananas without a few tarantulas, is very suspect by employees of the Produce Department.

Bananas imported from Central and South America are received in the Port of Houston, where they are warehoused for pick-up by tractor-trailers for OTR (over the road transport) to retail customers, large and small, all over the entire US. All that Mohammed had to do was to slip some cash to the "dockmaster" at the warehouses to open each crate of bananas, separate the "hands" of bananas, find the critters and gently push them into glass jars. The task was made easier, since Mohammed knew exactly which shipments of bananas contained the "extra" spiders he had paid for. Therefore, out of, say 1000 cases received, he only had to find and open , maybe 20. The Bill of Lading would identify exactly which cases had the "additional cargo". Mohammed had another Al Qaeda Agent performing that task for him. So, Part 2 of Phase One was well taken care of. There would be no screw-ups there, he was absolutely certain. Since tarantulas are VERY slow-moving creatures, the Agent had only to remove each "hand" of bananas (about 15 to each slatted-wooden case), shake it slightly, and the hairy little critters easily dislodged and fell to the bottom of the crate. They were then sort of gently pushed into a large glass jar with the help of a soft paint brush. It wasn't a difficult task, just tedius and time-consuming. He had a slight scare when another man came over to him and asked him "where's your knife?" "What knife - what are you talking about?" Back came, "Amigo, I didn't see anything - just do whatever it is you gotta do and get these crates off the dock. We got another shipment coming and I need the dock space for that load." There was another man standing nearby. The Agent asked him what he was doing just standing there. He said that the last time someone picked over bananas like that, he had cut a long slit down the length of selected bananas with a paring knife. The banana had been slit open in Mexico, stuffed with cocaine and carefully closed. At the warehouse, the banana was carefully slit open, again, since the original slit had grown closed in transit. The cylindrical plastic bag was removed, the "empty" banana was cut loose from the rest of the hand and trashed. The plastic bag was quickly stuffed into his pants pocket and the opened banana peel had the outward appearance of having been eaten by a hungry dock worker. "Nah, commented the Agent. I work for a small Importer and these bananas are going to a new client who doesn't understand that tarantulas are a common sight in crates of bananas. We wanted to remove them before the new customer FREAKED OUT." "Makes sense to me, Amigo. I don't see nuthin' around here. That way I don't have to worry about the Enforcers who will bust your legs and knees and crack your head with a baseball bat if they think you're seein' too much that don't concern you. You get to live a lot longer." "Hey", said the Agent, "that works for me. I'm finished and I'm outta here. Hasta la vista." "Da nada" and the two men went separate ways - the Agent with his gym bag with its Mason jars full of tarantulas. Another "mission accomplished".

From what Mohammed had already experienced, the third (and last) part of Phase One would be the easiest. The scorpions and the tarantulas had already been safely delivered and stored for the "ultimate Act" in preparation for his Grand Scheme. He went to a plain warehouse in the port area of Houston to collect his shipment of fleas and ticks. He knocked on the door of the Suite and it was shortly answered and opened. He identified himself as Consignee Mohammed Mahmoud, Importer, here to claim a box of insects for Laboratory Research. He presented the Government papers establishing his legitimacy for his shipment. His papers were taken and photocopied, for record purposes. He signed for the shipment - one small metal case, and it was released to him without comment. He shook hands with the man and thanked him, appropriately, though not effusively, turned, and departed the building with his box of flea and tick eggs. The last and final act of Phase One was now complete. Now to begin planning for Phase Two.

By now it was mid-September. Labor Day was past and Halloween was the next "observance". Now, Mohammed had to get really creative. He paid a visit to the Leasing Manager of the building and made a suggestion to him. How about a Contest for all of the commercial tenants of the building. Let's see who can have the most realistic Halloween decor in their Office spaces? Really deck out the place with spooky stuff. He could create a Committee of the Condo Owners, living in the floors above the Office Spaces to be the Judges. The winner would get half a month's rent free. The building Manager was VERY receptive and thought that was a great idea. Mohammed then rented a small storage room in a nearby facility. He arranged for the scorpions, tarantulas, tick and flea eggs to be delivered to the storage room by Special Courier. The room was Climate Controlled, so none of the eggs would start hatching. The scorpions and tarantulas were safely nestled in their boxes amid plenty of excelsior (basically very fine, thin, and long wood shavings of pine). He then went to a party store, which was already stocking ghoulish things for Halloween. He bought a couple of dozen large, black, rubbery spiders. He also bought several of those black plastic spider webs, and that wispy-filmy stuff used in haunted houses. Now it was time to wait until just before Halloween to spring his Great Surprise.

Phases One and Two were now complete.

HAPPY HALLOWEEN

All Trick and no Treat

Mohammed decided to spring his surprise on Halloween. By then all of the renovations to the Enron Building would be complete. All that would be left to do would be to find a way to get his creepy little critters into the building. The "phobia factor" was much greater than an actual bite or sting. Few people knew that a scorpion was actually quite small, even fully-grown, when a very large one was maybe 2 ½ inches long. The sting of a young one was not much more dangerous than that of a wasp. Even an adult specimen did not cause more discomfort than a rash on the skin about the size of an orange. Anti-toxin shots did n't help much. The rash would itch for a while and such as Calamine lotion would ease THAT. The rash would gradually disappear over the course of several days, leaving only a small scab at the site of the actual bite. The scab would remain until picked-off with such as a fingernail and white scar tissue about the size of a large pea would be the only reminder of the insect bite. A possible temporary side-effect would be some mild, involuntary muscle twitches, since the insect's toxin/venom was meant to attack either the victim's muscular system (the heart is the largest part of that), or respiratory system through the central nervous system (principally the lungs) causing temporary paralysis to varying degrees, since, in extreme cases, the lungs fail to supply enough oxygenated blood to the brain. However, the mere sight of the tiny, menacing-looking creature, with its tail curved up and forward along its back and tiny barb/stinger at the end, looked sinister enough. When frightened, the curved tail would be thrust rearward and downward, like a tiny whip, forcing the barb to penetrate the victim's skin. AND weren't the appearance of scary, sinister-looking things, albeit usually rubber, the whole point of Halloween, anyway? What better time to substitute the REAL creature for the black, rubber one? You could probably bring a whole box of rubber-looking tarantulas into a building and nobody would take any notice unless a few of them happened to move. The rubber ones move anyway if shaken only slightly. They are deliberately made to function in that way. If it doesn't move, it might as well be a black decal stuck to a window which wasn't very "Halloween-ish"

He had rented a small Apartment near Downtown Houston. He only needed it for a few months and he had sublet it from a tenant who was moving out before the end of the Lease. No Leases were bing renewed since the building, a high-rise, was being converted to Condominium Units. The "target market" was young Lawyers who needed both the convenience of living close to their Offices and proximity to Houston's Hobby Airport for travel to US Cities. For International flights, it wasn't a long cab ride to Houston's George W. Bush International Airport. Mohammed decided to go out for an early evening walk. He was passing a long line of parked cars when he noticed an enclosed pick-up truck that caught his attention. It had, emblazoned on both doors and the rear end, "K-9 Corps" - Police dogs. Suddenly it hit Mohammed like a ton of bricks - DOGS ! These were probably trained to sniff out drugs hidden in the floors or door panels of cars.. The truck had "Texas-Tax Exempt" tags on front and back. On closer look, the Driver's side windshield had decals on it just above the License sticker and the State Inspection sticker. One decal was "DEA" and the other was "INS". He glanced through the untinted passenger-side front window and noticed a short-waisted "Eisenhower-style", olive-drab jacket. A shoulder patch was visible and it read, "BORDER PATROL". All of this was interesting, but the thought that had occurred to Mohammed was DOGS. What is the bane of every dog? FLEAS and TICKS !!! What do fleas make their "host" do ? SCRATCH and Big Time. Fleas also jump and migrate quickly and easily. AND they lay eggs in the fur of their host. Mohammed would have to make time to find out who dealt with fleas on a regular basis. Kennels - Laboratories - where else ? He would have to find out. Additionally, ticks carried the dangerous and potentially deadly Lyme Disease. Two more "weapons" for his Campaign of Terror.

Getting fleas and ticks would require some ingenuity. He would have to find out who supplied research Laboratories with them. THAT would require setting up a "Front" Operation of some kind. The more "legitimate" his new business "Entity" appeared to be "on paper", the more success he would have in getting where he needed to be. Why not play the Federal Government AGAINST ITSELF, he mused. He had enough time to do some "thrashing around". He would apply to the Small Business Administration for a loan to start up his business. The Feds would never question a business they helped to finance. By the time anyone did an Audit, he would long-since have achieved his goal. His Application stated his Entity as " Scientific Research Supply, Inc." He was surprised that he was able to file his entire Application, on-line, using his laptop computer. The filing fee was nominal and he put it on his personal VISA Card. To Mohammed's total amazement, three days later, his Application showed up on his laptop as "APPROVED", AND, for ONE HUNDRED THOUSAND DOLLARS, which had already been electronically deposited into his PERSONAL checking account. He had no need for the money, but having it show up on his laptop as "US Treasury Deposit - Small Business Administration", IMMEDIATELY established the CREDIBILITY of his business. That had been the EASY part, to his surprise and amazement. NOW, came the hard part - to find out who raised fleas and ticks for sale and profit, and where they were located. THEN, he would have to rent a small Warehouse space to have the fleas and ticks delivered to the fictitious "Research Laboratory" and "properly" signed for. All of this had to be done without raising any suspicion by anyone - delivery drivers, watchmen, Security Guards, bystanders, casual observers - you name it. Mohammed would have to "baby-sit" the warehouse Office until the delivery was actually made and he signed-off on the POD (Proof of Delivery). None of this was particularly difficult, but it had to be closely and meticulously coordinated. Just one delivery box or carton left unattended on a warehouse doorstep because no one answered the knock or the doorbell quickly, could spell disaster. He would arrange to pee into a large, empty plastic bottle since he could not take the time and chance to go to the bathroom and miss the delivery.

Again, to his surprise and amazement, he found a Business that raised and sold fleas and ticks on the Internet. They were sold in only one quantity and he ordered three "Units". Additionally, the insects would have to be shipped as "live eggs" only by Special Courier, licensed to handle such cargo. Hatching time was said to be about a month and they were "packed" in excelsior, sealed in plastic. The eggs required very little oxygen to live and there was enough air trapped in the excelsior to survive a year or more. That suited Mohammed just fine, since the end of October, in Houston, would be cool enough to require the heat to be turned on in buildings. Flea and tick eggs were nearly invisible to the naked human eye and the three cartons of eggs would quickly hatch in the warmth of the building's air ducts. He would place the excelsior containing the eggs in an open-mesh net at the end of a broomstick, insert the stick as far as he could inside an air-duct-vent and shake it. The eggs would shake out of the excelsior and stick to the warm metal of the inside of the duct. The excelsior would remain in the net to be withdrawn along with the pole, thereby leaving no OBVIOUS evidence behind.

So far, there were no loose ends to have to keep track of and his Plan was falling into place nicely. Next, he paid a visit to the Office of the Leasing Agent and leased a small Office of roughly 1000 square feet. He ordered furniture and equipment he would likely never use. He leased it in the name of his agriculture Importing/Exporting Company, "Better Buys, Incorporated". It was a legitimate and viable enterprise and deliberately a little bit cryptic. That was for a purpose. He wanted to generate both curiousity and familiarity among his fellow tenants. He wanted nothing that even hinted at his Middle East connections and contacts. Although physically, he appeared to be Arabic, his pro-American Bio was beyond question. He was proud that his US-issued Passport showed dual American and British Citizenship and preferred to use it for identification purposes, even though he had a New York State Driver's License. His name was also on the Lease for the Apartment he shared in Paris, if Interpol, Scotland Yard, the Moussad, or anyone else cared to check him out. His Passport was full of Visa stamps for virtually every Country in Europe. He came and went Continentally and Inter-Continentally with both frequency and ease. THAT'S what folks engaged in the Import-Export business DID for a living. It was normal. It was logical. It was expected.. You either did it, or your competitors did it instead of you and THEY make the money you should be making. There were no international "Playboys" in the Import-Export business. Get caught screwing some broad in a sleazy hotel in London, Paris, New York, or Houston and find yourself a new line of work - maybe a pimp with a string of "loose" women in-tow. Then the Mafia was hot on your ass for invading their territory and interfering with one of their primary lines of work and sources of income. Mohammed wanted to be known by every tenant in the building. The Leasing Agency gave Mohammed a "ready-to-move-in" date of September First. That was perfect for his purposes. It would give him two full months to make full preparations and for the other tenants to get accustomed to his "comings and goings". He wanted THEM to consider HIM to be their welcome neighbor. Hopefully, that would place him above suspicion when his Plan was carried out. Even AFTER his Plan had been carried out, he would NOT immediately vacate. He would remain for as long as was necessary to carry out and complete his ruse. He needed to be one of the tenants who would complain most vociferously about "how could you allow such a terrible thing to happen"? IT would eventually be determined to have been a terrorist attack by Houston Authorities. That would allow the PERCEPTION that, first in New York City and then in Houston, the Government Authorities were incapable of protecting their citizens from Acts of Terrorism. Of course, the PERCEPTION(S)would be fallatious and without "basis-in-fact". However, Mohammed asked himself, both rhetorically and facetiously, WHEN did PERCEPTION mutate into and become REALITY? The answer was clear and unavoidable - when enough people really and firmly BELIEVED the PERCEPTION(S).

THAT, was part of the "definition of Terrorism". By extension, the populace rebels against both Government and Authority as-a-whole, in the form of street protests. Americans best remember this when it happened in the form of Vietnam War protests in the late 1960s and early 1970s. The protests were exacerbated by fringe, quasi-political groups such as the SDS, Black Panthers, Nation of Islam, and a whole host of lesser-known groups. Their combined efforts eventually turned the entire Country against the War and forced two Presidents from Office. Lyndon Johnson declined to run for re-Election. Richard Nixon resigned the Presidency under the threat of almost certain Impeachment. The end result was the Paris Peach Talks convened by Secretary of State Henry Kissinger and a Treaty that officially and formally ended the War. In protest to Government action or INACTION, dissatisfied Texans twice tried to resurrect and re-establish the Nation of the Republic of Texas. Independent Militias had formed in many States and Gun Dealers had done a brisk business, particularly in automatic and semi-automatic, hand-held, weapons, and assault rifles. Terrorism's ultimate goal was to cause rebellion through street- rioting leading to anarchy and the overall de-stabilization of State and Federal Government. In the short-term, the "attack" on the renovated Houston Enron Building had to be carried out to the point where the entire building had to be condemned as "unfit for human occupancy" and demolished.

The Big Event

Mohammed Mahmood did his best to make sure that the Halloween decorations in the Offices of the Ronne Tower would be fully appreciated by everyone in the surrounding buildings. They were even encouraged to come to the building on Halloween afternoon and vote for their favorite display. There would be ballot boxes with voting forms inside each office or Suite. The way Mohammed had figured it, the more people inside the building, the more effective his ploy would be. There would be panic with people running into one another and people falling to the floor. Some might suffer minor injuries, but, hopefully, nothing serious. To a terrorist Agent, fatalities were not the desired outcome. FEAR for one's life and safety were the "seeds to be planted in the minds of as many people as possible" was the real goal of TERRORISM. FEAR, UNCERTAINTY, DOUBT, PANIC, were the real desired outcome. Just like the immediate aftermath of the Japanese attack on Pearl Harbor on December 7, 1941, FEAR of anyone of Japanese ethnicity, who might have known or been complicit, overtook the entire United States. Japanese-Americans who were bona fide American Citizens, were rounded up and confined to "detention Camps" with the Federal Courts and the Constitution in full force. It had happened most recently with the bombing of the Alfred Murrah Federal Building in Oklahoma City. One hapless American citizen with an Arabic name had taken a flight to London immediately following the bombing. The FBI asked the British Scotland Yard and Interpol Police to detain the man upon his arrival in the UK. The man was subsequently cleared to continue his travel. Next, a man with an Arabic name, a Medical Doctor, was detained by the FBI on a train in Fort Worth, Texas, as it was about to leave the Station. The Doctor was eventually cleared to continue on his journey, however, not until he had been detained long enough to miss all of his connections on the way to his destination. Mohammed, therefore, had to protect himself against all of those possibilities. Namely, he had to place himself above all suspicions by local, State, and Federal Authorities.

As Halloween approached, he had to figure a "logical" way to get all of his "critters" into Ronne Towers. The biggest challenge would be getting his flea and tick eggs into the buildings HVAC ducts. As it would happen, that would turn out to be relatively easy.

He paid a visit to the office of the Building Manager. He was concerned that in the seasonal transition from air conditioning to heating, accumulated dust in the building's ductwork would inflame his allergies. He had medications to alleviate his coughing and sneezing, but was trying to wean himself off of them, since there were undesirable side effects. The Building Manager assured him that a duct cleaning would be performed. Would the Manager please give Mohammed a call a day or two ahead of the cleaning to ensure that it was done thoroughly and not just perfunctorily? "That is not a problem for me, Mr. Mahmood. I'd be glad to provide the scheduled time for their service of your

Office. In fact, I will instruct the site Supervisor to check-in with you both before and after his crew has serviced your office area." "Thank you so much, Sir. I DO thank you for your continued cooperation and the time you have devoted to my concerns." That would provide good "cover" for getting access to the HVAC ducts. Then, another stroke of luck occurred for Mohammed. He was having coffee in the building coffee shop when a group of women were abuzz over something at another table. He went over to them, introduced himself and asked what all the fuss was about. "You mean you haven't heard?" "Apparently not - heard what?" "The Manager of our bank was just fired. He was Pakistani and he let his business Visa expire and was deported. Federal Agents came for him yesterday afternoon and escorted him out in handcuffs. He went screaming Allah Akbar, whatever that means, and vowing revenge. There was also something about keeping an exotic pet without a proper Permit. We all knew he kept a Burmese Python snake in a glass cage in his Office. It was about four feet long and made us all rather creepy. It always seemed to be curled-up and sleeping. The manager said that was because he fed it two live rats a week, so it always had a full tummy which caused it to sleep. The Houston Humane Society came and took the snake away.

We're sorry he got deported, but he had no business keeping that snake in his Office. The building Manager STILL doesn't know about it. Apparently it was brought into the building in an ordinary gym bag and we all assumed it contained workout clothes. Front Desk Security Guard is supposed to check out that shit. He said he did once, but it turned out to contain plastic containers with cooked lunch food to be warmed in the microwave. He opened one container with rice and some kind of meat loaded with Middle Eastern strong spices. He told us that to him it stunk to high heaven. We knew since he used the microwave in the First Floor break room and the smell was so strong it would almost make you gag. We don't wish him any ill-will, but we're glad he's gone. We open tomorrow with a new Manager."

Ah, thought Mohammed, silently to himself. That guy is now the prime suspect when I spring my Halloween surprise. It doesn't get any better than this. He soon discovered that YES IT CAN get better for his purposes.

About a week before Halloween, the Building Manager called him to say that the HVAC duct cleaners would be coming in the morning. They would start at the top floor and work their way down to the Lobby. Mohammed met the crew upon its arrival and asked them if they would mind if he watched them work in just a few Offices. The had no objection. Mohammed wondered how in the world he was going to get his flea and tick eggs into the ducts on the end of his broomstick covered with a net to be shaken inside a duct? "Be patient" he mused to himself. Westerners wanted instant results and had no stomach for the long term. That was one of Al Qaeda's strengths. Like the North Vietnamese and the Viet Cong - first the French at DienBienPhu and later the Americans in South Vietnam, had no stomach for the "long road to victory". It was a simple matter of just being patient and waiting for the right time. The adversary would eventually "give up the fight and capitulate". Ten, twenty, thirty years to wait for ultimate success was just the price to be paid to first frustrate and then drive out your adversary. At the Office location of the second duct to be cleaned, Mohammed asked, "how's it going, guys." "This sucks, this just plain sucks. When will these idiots learn to replace the air filters once a month, at minimum? Go to the truck and get me at least two cases of new air filters. Then note in the Recommendations Section of the Work Order, that two new air filters be on-hand for the Client on an on-going basis. Now, lets start replacing every goddamned air filter in whole fucking building. Put the new filters in the HVAC room until after we've cleaned out the entire air duct system.. We'll store them all there and take them out as we need them." Mohammed asked, "you mean I can't take out the new filters for just my Office now and do it myself?" "Oh, no, sir, it will take all day to suck out the dead air and any debris from the building's ducts. We won't start replacing filters until at least tomorrow." It was all "music to Mohammed's ears". He pretended to work late, until the duct cleaners had left for the day. Then he took his wooden box, full of excelsior and imbedded flea and tick eggs down to the HVAC Room and proceeded to "infest" each and every new air filter with the eggs, which would not hatch for a week to ten days. They would literally be blown out of the filters and into the ducts by warm, incoming "polluted" air that would be trapped by the filters, one particulate at a time. If anyone were to even remotely suspect what had happened, it would be blamed on Quality Control wherever the supplier kept his inventory of new air filters. No chance of any trace back to Mohammed Mahmoud. All of this did, however give him a thought.

Getting the tarantulas into the building would be relatively easy - it was just a matter of the right timing. He decided not to place all the scorpions

INSIDE the building. They were small and easily frightened. If he were to be just a little bit careless in his haste and handling of them, HE might be bitten. In their natural habitat, they were creatures of the outdoors. He would wait until after dark and then drop them all in the grass and shrubbery surrounding the building. He had enough of them to spread some around adjacent buildings. It was then that he had another thought - the underground parking garage. It tended to get hot down there and a lot of folks often left their car window's open just a few inches. It was not enough for a thief to get his hand inside the car and pull up the lock button to open the car door, but enough to drop in a scorpion. The critter would crawl up a man's pant leg or go under a woman's skirt. What an ideal environment for such as a scorpion - soft skin, warm inner legs and thighs. If the man was wearing boxer shorts, the critter would crawl inside. The man would reach down to scratch the annoyance. The scorpion would react defensively and throw his barbed tail-stinger into the man's penis or testicle. It would, of course, initially sting. Within a few minutes the pain would become severe. The man would become preoccupied and lose control of his car and probably cause a wreck, not far from downtown Houston. If a woman driver happened not to be wearing a girdle, pantyhose, or panties and felt the irritation or intrusion into her pubic area, whether hirsute or clean-shaven, she would reach down and rub her crotch. That would frighten the scorpion and initiate the same sting. The end result would be the same as for the male driver - panic and loss of control of the vehicle. Either way it would achieve the desired results for Mohammed. That solved the problem of where to place the scorpions. That left only the matter of the tarantula spiders.

Mohammed returned to the site of the best "intelligence" he had for the building - the ground floor coffee shop. The usual crowd of Office Staff was there. It was just a few days until Halloween. He heavily promoted the Building Manager's idea of a Contest for the best Office decorations. "Remember, half a month of free rent for the winning decoration." The ladies were really looking forward to the Event and the Contest. It would really be a nice change of their daily routine. Mohammed said, "now ladies, I'm going to show you something and I want you to promise me that you will not freak-out or anything, okay?" They all agreed to stay calm. He reached into his suit coat pocket and produced a large, black, very hairy, wiggly, rubber tarantula spider. It was about the size of a glass coaster. He held it up in his hand and it was larger than the palm of his hand. Since all of them had been forewarned, none of them panicked. "Recently, I've heard some of you mention that you planned to hang fake spider webs from the ceilings, cabinets and lamps in your Offices. Well, I ask you, what's a spider web without a resident spider? Since I'm going to have a few webs in my Office, also, I went to a local Party Store and bought some big, hairy, black-rubber spiders. Consider it my contribution to your Offices for the fun of the Halloween Contest."

"Thank you so much, Mr. Mohammed, for your thoughtfulness. We had exactly the same idea, but we didn't know where to find such a store and we did not want to spend our entire lunch hour shopping for such things, even if we knew where to go. This is so thoughtful of you. What do we owe you for this - I mean, we don't want to insult you, but nothing is free and our Offices DO have a fund for this sort of thing, sooooo." "Not to worry or concern yourselves, ladies. It is my pleasure to be able to be of assistance to you, and may the best and spookiest office display win the Halloween Contest."

Mohammed's final task was how to get the actual, live, tarantula spiders into the individual Offices. THAT would take some doing, incredible timing and incredible luck, not be caught in the act of doing it. Mohammed went back to his Office when the telephone rang. It was the Building Manager telling him to be at a meeting in the Front Office at 9:00 the next morning. The City of Houston's Assistant Fire Chief would conduct a briefing and review the building's fire evacuation plan. It was a MUST ATTEND meeting of all Building tenants and their entire Staffs. All of their Office telephones were to be put on automatic answering machines, no exceptions. The Building Manager, after the meeting, would host a "coffee, Danish, and donut, get-to-know-your-fellow-tenant" reception. All attendees were strongly encouraged to attend, although it was not required. Another stroke of incredibly good luck for Mohammed. He was absolutely certain that all of the Office Managers and their entire Staffs would attend the reception. He would be able to politely excuse himself and tend to the business of placing his live tarantula spiders into the Offices, desk drawers, and purses of every tenant. Most all Secretaries would leave their purses in their Offices and carry their cell phones in cases on their belts or waistbands.

The meeting went exactly as planned and nobody left the reception early except Mohammed. He took the elevator straight to his Office where he had left his gym bag, inside of which were the many small plastic containers holding one tarantula spider each. He grabbed the bag and took the elevator straight to the top floor. He would begin there, or so he thought. Stepping out of the elevator, the hall lights immediately went out and flood lights mounted high on the wall came on. Just to the side of the lights, a small red light had come on. Mohammed knew that meant that either a security motion detector or an infra-red heat detector was focused on him. Reacting instinctively, he snapped his fingers and threw both arms into the air and uttered aloud, "damn, I got off on the wrong floor", in case the sensor also had audio. He attempted to get back on the elevator, but the doors had already closed behind him. He pressed the DOWN button, but it would not activate. He did not relish the idea of going down the stairs, so he figured he would just bide him time and wait. The large, red, fire alarm bell, high on the wall had not gone off, so he just sat down on the floor and leaned against the wall and waited. He heard a motor begin to hum and the elevator doors slowly opened. Several tenants he recognized from the Fire Chief's meeting stepped out. "What's going on" asked Mohammed? One lady said, "the Chief decided to end the Meeting with a walk-through of the entire building, checking on fire alarms, smoke detectors, and making sure that all fire extinguishers were operable and had their inspection tags current. We all think its BS, but we have no choice but to play along and do as he asks." "Shit", Mohammed said silently to himself, there goes my plan to place the tarantulas. Wait a minute, he mused to himself, maybe and maybe not. He'll just have to scale-down his plan with the spiders, just a bit. He Already had his 'cover' in place with the Bank Manager kicked out and vowing revenge/reprisal. He'd just go to the nearest Krispy Kreme donut shop on Halloween morning and pick up a box of donuts for every Office in the Building. There couldn't be more than 50 Offices in the Building and he would personally treat each tenant to donuts. At each Office, he'd engage in small talk and wait for a distraction, such as a need to send or receive a Fax or make copies, or make a trip to the ladies' room. In each box with donuts, would be one or two plastic containers, each with a spider inside. It all went amazingly smoothly. He only needed a few "unguarded" seconds to open a Staffer's desk drawer, pop-off the plastic lid, invert the small container and shake out the spider into the drawer. In a few cases, he had more time when the Staffer went to make copies in another room. Then, he would locate her handbag, open the top and drop in the spider. He had 30 spiders and "placed" them all in less than an hour, total, with, of course, his Halloween "treat" of Krispy Kreme donuts. Now, all he had to do was return to his Office and wait. Hours went by and he heard nothing. He decided to go to lunch. On the way back from lunch, he decided to stop in at the Lobby Coffee Shop for the latest news/gossip. He recognized Linda and asked if anything was new. She told him, " some idiot or prankster put a tarantula in my desk drawer. I guess he thought it would freak me out, or something. Well, I was raised on a ranch outside of Houston and I'm used to such critters. On sight, they look creepy and nasty, but they're really quite friendly. It crawled into my palm and up my arm. I took the Tupperware I had my lunch in, removed the lid and he crawled right into it. It had a little leftover salad inside and he seemed to like that. I put the lid back on. You know, Mr. Mohammed, they don't need much air to live on. I'll take it home and my son will take it to school to the Science Lab where they'll put it in a large tank with sand, snakes, iguanas, and the like and it will be right at home. Nobody in the entire building had any problem with his spiders. Most of the tenants just opened a window to the outside and shook the spiders off their hand or arm. "Bummer", thought

Mohammed, to himself. Maybe he'd have better luck with the scorpions, ticks, and fleas. He'd just have to wait and find out. No, he would not wait. He had a plan and he needed to stick to it. He had a new idea with the leftover scorpions. Who said they had to be placed in Offices? He had almost overlooked the bathrooms that open to the hallway on each floor. Then, and idea hit him. All bathrooms need toilet paper which comes on a roll. He'd partially unravel several rolls of toilet paper and remove enough paper to create a small cavity of maybe an inch square and deep, just like hollowing out a book to hide a weapon or whatever. He'd then place inside one scorpion and carefully replace the unraveled panels of paper back onto the roll. He could do all of that in the privacy of his Office, and he did just that. It was then an easy task to go into each Men's Room, enter each stall, remove the roll that was on the holder, and replace it with a roll he'd altered. Nobody was EVER careful about how they removed panels of toilet paper from the roll. They's just grab the front panel and use it to spin the entire roll to remove about two feet of paper. The spinning roll would agitate the critter inside . It would come flying from its little hole and probably land on the thigh of the toilet's occupant where it would quickly insert it's toxic barb. Mohammed only had to make sure that the panels came off the roller from the top and not the bottom. Otherwise, the critter would be thrown against the side wall of the stall and probably be smashed. Also, how was he going to manage to get the Ladies' Room unoccupied for a couple of minutes? That could prove very difficult without attracting attention and suspicion. Just then, he had a most welcome surprise. Office doors opened and Staffers came rushing out in to the hall. "What's going on", he asked one of the ladies? "Oh, some crap about a practice fire evacuation of the building down into the Lobby. They're going to cut off all non-essential power to the building to see how well we can get down there without the elevators and emergency hallway lights only. We're not supposed to run and clog the staircases". "Thanks for the 'heads-up'", he told the lady. He waited a few minutes for the hallway to clear out and then entered as many restrooms as he could with the critters he had left hidden inside the paper rolls. Fortunately, he had a little pen light flashlight inside his gym bag. Job done, he hurried to join the rest of the evacuees. Upon reaching the Lobby, the Fire Marshall asked him what the hell took him so long. As he was hurrying down the staircase, he clumsily caught the heel of his shoe on the edge of a stair riser and tripped and fell. It just knocked the wind out of him, so he sat down on a landing to catch his breath and check out his body parts to make sure nothing was broken. His ankle was a little sore from having been twisted, but he'd just wear an Ace Bandage on it for a couple of days and was sure he'd be OK. The Fire Marshall snapped at him, "I thought I told all of you to slow down, take it easy, not to panic and proceed down the floors in an order ly fashion?" "Sorry, Sir, I did the best I could." "Okay, then, go over to that desk and initial the Master Building Roster so we can be sure the building is fully cleared of all occupants." Mohammed threw him a sloppy mock salute, and did what he was told to do. NOW, FINALLY, all of the details had been attended to and accomplished. It was WAITING TIME, and that was the part Mohammed hated the most, since he tended to be impatient and despised "unknowns". Mohammed left for the day and went to the parking garage to get his car AND to check on the possible early results of the scorpions he had planted earlier. He found a lady with her back up against the front of what he presumed to be her car. There was a man with her. He went over to them and asked if anything was wrong. Both looked a bit pale. She was complaining about abdominal pain, nausea, and mild cramps in her leg. He saw where she had already vomited on the floor of the garage and was trying to drink some water from a plastic bottle she kept in her purse. The man was messaging her lower leg in an attempt relieve the cramp. He suddenly stood up, turned his head to the side and vomited as he clutched his stomach with both hands. She already ruled out menstrual cramps. The man put both of his hands flat on the hood of the car, bent over and said he might pass out. He looked as white as a sheet. He felt something on the back of his neck and swatted at it with his hand. A scorpion, about an inch and a half long landed on the hood of the car, close to where his head hung down. "Oh, shit, I know what THAT is. How the hell did it get down here? They're usually only found in desert sand." "What IS it, asked the lady?" "It's a fucking scorpion - that's what it is. Now I know why we both feel like crap. It doesn't bite, it's barbed tail penetrates the skin and injects a non-lethal venom. It hurts like a son-of-a-bitch, but the reaction is delayed as the venom travels from a capillary just under the skin, into main blood stream. Kinda like a mosquito bite that doesn't itch for a while after the first little sting." "Will we be OK" asked the lady? "Oh yeah, but you'll need to get off your feet as soon as you can. You won't want to eat for a while and don't try to force yourself, 'cause you'll toss it up as soon as it hits your stomach and you may experience the dry-heaves for a while. Not very pleasant, but far from deadly and you'll probably feel weak as a kitten for a while until your white blood cells neutralize the toxin in the venom. The barbed stinger on its tail is extremely small and cannot deliver much venom in one thrust. Fortunately for us, this one is quite small and, therefore, young and it's venom is not very strong." "Will I be able to drive my car home?" "Lady, that's your call to make. The cramps in your calf muscles will still allow you to press the brake and the gas with sufficient force from your foot to stop and start, but you'll need to drive very defensively, as in leaving lots of room between you and the vehicle in front of you so you can hit the brake the brakes several times if your calf muscle cramps up on you again. Also, if you have an attack of lightheadedness, you won't be able keep yourself from passing out for a few minutes which means you'll lose control of your car and probably have wreck your car or cause an accident with one or more other cars. Normally, if you feel dizzy, you can bend way over and place your head between your legs so that gravity will keep the flow of blood going to your brain and prevent you from passing out, HOWEVER, you'll be stuck behind the steering wheel and seat-belted in to prevent you from doing just that. Also, don't forget the nausea thing. If you start having the dry-heaves in spasms, which is normal, you'll spray stomach acid on your clothes, on the instrument panel, dashboard and windshield. Your natural tendency will be to turn your head toward the passenger seat to try to contain the mess. When you do so, you have no choice but to lower your head and take your eyes off the road and probably have an accident or cause a pile-up. Why take the chance? Leave your car here tonight and call your husband or a friend or neighbor to come take you home. If you are too embarrassed, give me the number and I'll call for you on my cell phone." "Just who or what are you, anyway?" "I'm Robert , uh, 'Bob' Hartwell. I'm an MD. I work for a Life Insurance Company with an Office in the RONNE Building. I review applications for Life Insurance to determine whether or not issued Policies should be Rated for medical reasons." "Okay, but how do you know so much about creepy things like scorpions?" "Okay, here goes - basic anatomy is the same in ALL living things. All of the same organs are there in the various species, just configured differently in non-humans. Most of snake is just under its back except for its stomach, which takes up most of its body, especially just after it has eaten. I also took an Elective Course in my last year of Med School. It was "serpantology" which pertains to things that bite or squeeze to kill or subdue/paralize prey (not road kill or carrion) long enough to either eat it alive or suck all of the body fluids from it. That had always fascinated me and still does, to this day. Some, like the scorpion, use their sting as a defense mechanism to slow you down or stop you long enough for them to get away from what, to them, is a threat to their life. Ie: you frightened or startled them and they just want to get away from you and fast and get on with their normal, daily routine, which is, most likely, looking for food more their size. An adult human being looming high over a tiny scorpion is quite a formidable sight. There, so now you know HOW I KNOW." "Dr. if you're trying to either make me feel better or lay a guilt trip on me about scaring a tiny insect into stinging me, it ISN'T working." "Okay, but you'll have to admit that my scholarly explanation of what has happened to the both of us has taken your mind off your stomach and leg. That's called "psychosomatic" - if your mind tells you you're going to feel better, you probably will - mind over matter, is the layman's expression. Now let's tend to the matter of getting you home - ah, I've got it - I'll drive you home in my car." "But you got bitten, too and might have the same problems with driving YOUR car." "Ah, yes, that is true, BUT, you forget that I am a Doctor and in the back seat of my car is my black bag full of medicinal goodies. Besides, I'll have you next to me as my Co-Pilot. I'll gladly chance it. SO, now that THAT's settled, I can address to myself, the larger question." "Which IS?" "Look, lady, all critters of the wild have relatives and probably offspring. Scorpions are NOT 'territorial' which is to say no dominant male to protect his harem, if you will." "Could the whole building be infested with them, Doctor?" "Not likely. There'd be precious little food for them and they'd be far from their natural environment. I'd bet my Medical License that the one that bit us did not come from inside the building. It probably came from the grass outside and crawled into something like the wheel well of our cars. Then it crawled out and up our shoes to our leg where the flesh is warm and soft. When we took a step or two, our legs moved/vibrated and scared it into biting us. We'll know soon enough, when the landscapers come to pull up the summer flower plantings and replace them seasonal pansies and chrysanthemums. If that's where this scorpion came from, the men working on the gardens will all be bitten and panic. We'll just have to wait and see." Mohammed, sensing the man and woman didn't need his help, had moved away, but not very far - he was still within hearing distance and heard every word of what the lady and the doctor had said. N ow he had "professional corroboration" for his decision to infest the gardens and shrubbery around the Building with his scorpions. He got into his car and drove to his apartment and turned on the evening traffic news to hear if there had been any nasty accidents in the Houston area. There had been none, other than the usual on Houston's busy Freeways.

Wait a minute, Mohammed thought to himself. What am I doing? I think I have forgotten what it is that I came to accomplish. I didn't come here to cause death and destruction. I came here as a terrorist, to cause the people in this building to want to leave it, PERMANENTLY. I want the City of Houston, one of the largest in the US, to have to condemn this building as "unfit for human habitation" and cause it to be demolished. That was the REAL goal of destroying the World Trade Center towers in New York - not to destroy it, necessarily, but to cause such terror that all of the occupants of the building to refuse to work inside it. Without the rental revenue of their occupancy of its space, it would become an unprofitable investment. Even with the tax writeoff of vacant spaces, after a few years of nothing more than "straight-line depreciation", it could only be sold to some Government Agency using tax dollars. That was not likely. As a last resort, maybe some Arab Country rich with "petro-dollars", would buy it, but even that was unlikely.

The WTC twin towers were destroyed as an act of pure egotism by his terrorist brother, Mohammed Atta. The act of doing so had only the "incidental approval" of Osama bin Laden, as he was informed of it by his Lieutenants. Osama had said, purportedly, basically, "okay, give it a try and let's see what happens". Mohammed Atta had planned the rental truck explosion in the underground parking garage of the WTC using nitrate fertilizer, sometime earlier, but it was not powerful enough. Atta had thought that the reverberation of sound from the explosion would cause the concrete from the supporting pillars to crumble and separate from the rebar, but the truck had been parked too far away from the bulk of the pillars. The explosion shock wave had dissipated too much to cause any real damage. After THAT failure, Atta had gotten his ego involved and had vowed that the WTC towers WOULD be destroyed, whatever it might take. Mohammed Mahmoud would not make that mistake - he was a "professional" terrorist and he would not allow his ego to become involved and pervert the true meaning of Islam according to the Supreme One - Allah. Allah's will WOULD be done and with minimal loss of life - preferably with no loss of life. Stupid Ones kill - ingenious Ones simply terrify by severely disrupting daily life among average people and causing doubt as to whether Officials can adequately protect them and their loved ones from their fears, both inside and outside of their homes.

Had it been up to Mohammed, when the WTC Towers had been destroyed, all of the appropriate elected Officials would have issued a joint statement: "Okay, Osama, you won this round. We are going to rebuild these twin towers exactly according to the original blueprints and WE DARE YOU TO TRY IT AGAIN. You have not defeated us, you have merely AROUSED A SLEEPING GIANT and you will come to severely regret having done so. We will make you pay and you will pay dearly." Given the opportunity, that's what Mohammed would have told America. It would have caused a temporary setback for Al Qaeda and caused it to adjust it's aims and goals. Instead, the Americans simply admitted defeat and made a hollow , meaningless vow of some sort of nebulous revenge. They invaded Iraq and deposed Saddam Hussein when they should have invaded the Bora Bora region of Afghanistan where they MIGHT have found bin Laden.

Mohammed mentally chastised himself for wishing traffic accidents on the highways of Houston. He had temporarily forgotten his true mission, which was to cause Houston authorities to condemn the Ronne building as infested with fleas and ticks. No amount of treatment of any kind would entirely clear the whole building of the pesky insects, at least to the satisfaction of present and future tenants and Residents of the Condos. If the Exterminators did not realize that the infestation came solely from the building's many air filters and immediately replace all of them and then re-clean all of the ducts, they would never entirely rid the building of its infestation. The Manager might PROCLAIM the building to be insect-free, but the stigma would always remain. With no tenants or owners, alarm systems and power would be turned off. Eventually, windows would be broken to gain entry by vagrants. They would resort to unsafe cooking devices for their meals (charcoal or propane grills). There would be no City water available to put out any such fires. Plastic-bottled water and soft drinks would cause trash to pile up and drunks would become a big problem. The City would be forced to condemn the building and let Contracts to demolish it.

THE AFTERMATH
- THE FALLOUT

To Mohammed's dismay, the panic he had hoped for with his spiders and scorpions did not materialize. The scorpions were very small and most folks did not even recognize them for what they were. The few that got on arms or legs were swatted away with the sweep of a hand or the flick of a finger before they had a chance to plant their toxic venom with their barbed tail. When they landed on the floor they were easily squashed by a shoe. Those he had placed inside the rolls of toilet paper had stung a few ladies, but no men. Those that had landed on ladies sitting on the commode were swatted off on to the floor and squashed. There was one incident with a lady being stung high up on the inside of her right thigh where the flesh was warm,soft and moist. She flicked it off and squashed it with her shoe and did recognize what it was. She had calmly finished her "business" and walked directly back to office and called 911. She then took the elevator to the Lobby and met the arriving ambulance in front of the building. She stepped into the back of it and got nothing more than a tetanus shot, some neosporin ointment to rub-in on the site of the tiny sting and a small, round bandaid. So much for Mohammed's Halloween surprise. At least nobody had the slightest clue that Mohammed was the person responsible. Then, two things happened concurrently - one inside the building and the other outside of the building. The lawn care guys came to give the lawn one last cut for the year. Several of them were bitten by some scorpions on their sandaled feet. None recognized what had bitten them and assumed it was mosquitos. They "danced around a bit" from the sting and muttered something in Spanish which no one who understood Spanish was willing to translate. Their Crew Leader saw the Building Manager and demanded that the grounds be sprayed for insects before they cut the grass in the Spring. They WOULD finish this cut unless something more dangerous was discovered, like a snake.

The entire building had pre-programmed thermostats. The Master Unit in the HVAC Room in the Lobby started the natural gas furnaces and each individual Unit in the Offices and Condos came on, automatically, on November First. If it turned out to be unseasonably warm on that date, there was a way to override individual Units, but it had to be done manually by Building Maintenance, and only by individual request. Some tenants considered that to be an inconvenience, but the whole system operated much more efficiently and at much lower cost if the entire building converted over at the same time. Each Unit had three Modes - Off, Air Conditioning, Heat. Only the Off Mode could be entered, manually, by an individual Unit. If that Mode was selected, that Unit would be immediately shut down, but there was a 24-hour waiting period while that particular Unit's thermostat "recycled itself". Then, only Maintenance could restore that Unit to it's Automatic Mode. That was done to avoid a power surge to the motors in the Units. If too many Units went from one Mode to another in a short period of time (usually within an hour), the power surge, particularly for Air Conditioning, would overwhelm the whole System. Lights might begin to flicker and computers might crash. It was sort of like the power surge from a lightning strike to the building, though on a lesser scale, voltage-wise. However, in the case of a thermostat power surge, it was not enough of a "jolt" to trigger the surge protectors that most folks used to protect their computers. It would not "fry" a computer, but it probably would cause a computer to need to be rebooted. It might also wipe-out some Data on a Spreadsheet program receiving new information input. That which had already been saved to memory was probably safe. However, new "lines of data input" that had not been saved to memory, line-by-line, were probably at risk. It would not be long before the insect eggs, many already in the larva stage, in the air filters, would begin to hatch and grow into adults. Incoming, dirty air would be cleansed in the filters and blown out into the ducts and, along with it, eggs and larva. The warmed ducts from the natural gas jets in the Master HVAC Unit in the room in the Lobby, would cause the entire duct system to be infested. The same air flow that had cleansed the incoming, "recycled" air through the filters, would blow out the eggs, larva, and mature fleas and ticks through the fresh air "registers" in each Unit in the entire building. Mohammed wondered if the sudden influx of the pests would be too obvious. His apprehension was soon put to rest with an announcement from Building Management. Several occupants of the Condos who were permitted to have pets in their Units, were informed by Building Management that their veteranians had not yet provided written proof of flea and tick treatment, as required by their Unit Maintenance Agreement. Those with pet dogs or cats were told to get their animals treated immediately, or they would have to board their pets with a kennel until their pets had been treated. What a stroke of good fortune, Mohammed thought. NOW, if fleas or ticks were to be discovered within the building, it would be blamed on the pet owners who had not yet provided the Manager with written proof of treatment.

It wasn't very long before fleas and ticks began appearing in Offices throughout the building. Men and women were scratching themselves in unseemly anatomical places. The fleas were annoying enough. The ticks were quite another matter. First, they were literally blood suckers. They literally buried their tiny heads into skin to feed off capillary blood and engorge their tiny bodies. Unlike fleas, ticks carried the potentially life-threatening Lyme disease. Their brown bodies, normally very flat, became rounded as they engorged themselves on either animal or human blood. For those not familiar with them, they are easy to pull off the skin with the thumb and forefinger. However, usually, in doing so, their tiny head is separated from their body and is left buried in the skin. When left there, the head decomposes and causes an infection which does not go away unless treated by a physician. To make matters much worse, the usual site of tick attachment to the human body is the underarms and the crotch. Both areas are normally warm, soft, and protected by clothing. The only effective "on site" treatment for tick removal is lie on one's back and raise one's arms over one's head (if the underarm is where the tick has buried itself). Another person must light a paper match (not a lighter), and place the flame very close to where the head of the tick is buried into the skin. The heat from the lighted match will cause the tick to back out its head, and then can be safely removed. If the site of the attached tick is the crotch, the procedure is the same, but is complicated by both the greater sensitivity of the area and the probable presence of some density or thickness of pubic hair. Obviously, if the infected person is very hirsute in that area, the application of a lighted match presents complications. If the "victim" is female, she must carefully pull back the hair to expose the skin in the area immediately around the tick. Then the flame of the match is applied until the tick backs its head out of the skin. It usually takes two people to do this and preferably the "assisting" person is also female. The victim pulls aside the hair and locates the tick, while the other person lights and applies the flame of the match to the tender skin near the buried head of the tick, being careful NOT to burn the head of the tick and sever it from the rest of the tick's body. There aren't too many people willing to undergo the procedure while on their back, naked, on a desk or couch. The same procedure must be undergone by males, but the privacy issue is usually less of a problem. A guy will usually simply bear the momentary pain of the lighted match and tell the assisting person to "get on with it and get that damned thing out of me and be damned sure to get all of the critter - head too." The complicating factor (s) for a male are the EXTERNAL presence of the penis and the scrotum, both of which are EXTREMELY tender and sensitive. For either gender, intercourse is usually too painful for a couple of days, even with the application of some skin-soothing medication. Most people avoid going to the Emergency Room in a Hospital, since the automatic first step is for an Aide or Orderly to shave the entire pubic area while being careful not to touch the tick itself. Sometimes, a small piece of gauze soaked in rubbing alcohol and held to the skin and tick, will cause the tick to unattach itself needing air to breathe (the alcohol blocks all air getting to the tick. It's needs for air are minuscule, but it does need some air and the alcohol blocks ALL air to the tick). However, Mohammed knew that very few people who were not physicians, were aware of the "field method of tick removal", much less the need to do so before the tick was bloated with blood to the size of a garden pea. If the tick got that big, it would disengage itself from the skin, leaving behind its infection. There were rumors that several ladies had found ticks on various parts of their anatomy. Apparently, they knew it was a tick and chose to leave it alone until they got home and have their husbands tend to removing it. How long would it be before it was clear that the entire RONNE Building was infested? Mohammed had no idea, nor, at this point, did he much care. He had planted his "seeds" of doubt . As any "farmer" would know, it was now up to events and circumstances for the seeds to either "flower" or die, for whatever reason.

Mohammed learned that the Doctor and lady from the scorpion bite in the parking garage, the Doctor had driven her home, both had arrived safely at the lady's home. For that he was grateful. It was not Al Qaeda's intent to cause extreme harm or death. Their goal was to cause doubt, within the Citizenry, of its Government's ability to protect them and provide them with a safe environment within which to live, work, and, yes, pursue pleasurable, outside interests, such as attend sporting events, Concerts, artistic displays, whatever. Mohammed Mahmood was a "purist". Mohammed Atta had been an Opportunist and not a Purist. Yes, he had succeeded with his death and destruction. By doing so, he had perverted the message of true Islam. Mohammed would not follow the same path. He would continue to plants the seeds of unrest and doubt. He would not participate in wanton, willful death just to prove he had the ability to do so. True Islam did not approve of that and neither would THAT provide a clear path to Eternal Life through Allah - the One True God.

There had been reports and complaints of an infestation of fleas in many of the Offices in the building. Exterminators had been called and all

Offices had been treated, to the satisfaction of all occupants. "Bummer" thought Mohammed. Then came back the Houston Fire Chief. He ordered an immediate evacuation of the entire building. A natural gas leak had been detected by a sensor in the Lobby. It had sent an automatic signal to the local Fire Station. An inspection had disclosed that a critical valve in the HVAC Room in the Lobby had been opened ever so slightly. How did that happen, the Fire Chief wondered? Natural gas pipe fittings and valves were, by City Code, required to be tight enough that a common pair of pliers would not be enough to open one. Although the valve handle was small enough that it could theoretically be twisted open with one or both hands, in reality, It could not and nobody had a hand grip strong enough to turn the valve. The Gas Company had a special, much larger valve handle with a special clamp that allowed it to be placed on top of the smaller handle. The larger handle, when affixed, allowed much greater torque to be applied to the valve with the use of both hands. It was then that the Chief noticed something small, but significant. The valve and fittings were all made of brass, a relatively soft metal. There was no way that one person could have placed enough of a grip on the valve handle, even using both hands. He took out his flashlight and shined it on the brass fitting immediately under the valve handle. That fitting connected the handle to the larger pipe below which controlled the actual flow of gas through the larger pipe. That brass fitting was hexagonal and was slightly "scratched or scored" on opposite sides. Someone had used a common vice-grip, slip-joint, or pipe wrench to provide enough torque to turn that valve. However, they had not used it on the valve itself. Instead, they turned the brass coupling just below the valve handle to open the valve itself. Gas had been seeping out for quite some time but in low enough quantities as to not be easily detected by a person's sense of smell. The entire building was ordered vacated, indefinitely, or at least until the cause of the valve tampering had been determined. On a wild hunch, the Chief searched the entire HVAC Room by himself. In one corner, stacked on top of one another were six cardboard boxes of new air filters. As he removed each box from the stack, he checked to see if it was sealed or had been opened. All were sealed shut except the bottom box. Its flaps had been opened. The new filters were standing on their ends. He pulled each one out, maybe an inch and looked between them, but they were too tightly packed together to see all the way to the bottom of the box. He decided to replace the ones he had pulled up a bit and pushed them back down. Funny thing, they didn't seem to want to go back in neatly. He didn't want to have to remove them all and repack the box. He tapped the entire box with the toe of his shoe to try to get the protruding filters to fall back into place in the box. None of the filters moved. "Ah shit", he muttered to himself. "I don't have time today to be farting around with a stupid box of air filters". Then he got his ego into it and pulled out of the box every damned filter. He gazed down into the empty box and there it was, plain as day, just staring at him - a long-handled pair of slip joint pliers with teeth that appeared to match the scratches on the brass pipe fitting. "Well whatta ya know", he almost yelled out. He had found the "weapon" used to cause the gas leak. Instinctively, he pulled a pair of rubber gloves from his right rear pocket and put them on before he picked up the slipjoints although it did no good since the entire handle of the tool had been scored in a pattern for better grip. One of the Secretaries from the bank across the Lobby saw the Chief with the tool in his hand and quipped, "hey Chief, I guess they don't pay you enough to be Fire Chief, so you gotta moonlight as a plumber?" "Something like that", shot back the Chief. "No, seriously, I found the source of the gas leak. You wouldn't happen to kn ow who these big pliers belong to, do you?" "Well, I can't say for sure since I don't know much about tools, but they look like what the fired Manager of our Bank used to keep in his Office. He said he used them to adjust the back rest on his desk chair and used them a couple of times to tighten the battery cables un der the hood of his car." "Can you tell my what he got fired for?" "Sure, one day some men from the Houston Police, the FBI and the INS came in and arrested him and hauled him off in handcuffs. Said he was in the US on a expired Business Visa. He was from Pakistan, I think, and was one royally pissed-off guy when he left. Shouted something about Allah Akbar on the way out the door and into a Police car. That's the last I ever saw of him." "These are forensic evidence which I cannot discuss, pending a full investigation, but I'd have to say it looks like he tried to set the whole building ablaze by tempering with the main natural gas valve to cause a steady, low-level leak." "Oh, mygosh, Chief, I just remembered that some of the tenants were bitten by fleas and ticks and the building has been sprayed to kill them. Building Manager thinks they may have come in with some of the dogs and cats owned by those in the Condos. However, there may be some guys who got tick-bit. The recommended method of removal of the ticks is to burn the skin near their imbedded heads with a match. That's supposed to cause the tick to remove his head from the skin. I don't know if anybody is actually doing that, but striking a match could cause an explosion, couldn't it?" "Damned right it could and there goes the entire building." "Lady, please do me a favor and go get the Building Manager to come here, right now." "You got it, Chief". "Sir, I don't have time to explain right now, but I need you to somehow get every tenant in the entire building to open all of their windows to the outside immediately. You've had a low-level natural gas leak in the building for some time now. We've got to get all of that gas vented to the outside as soon as possible. Until then, any possible source of ignition could leave your whole building in a heap of rubble." The Condo occupants were furious to have to relocate at least temporarily. The Business tenants all had to notify their Home Offices of the evacuation. Almost all of the business tenants were told by their Home Offices to move out permanently and find new quarters. Now, with the building only half occupied, security became an issue with the Condo owners who served notice of intent to sell their Units.

A group of Asian investors filed notice of intent to buy the building "as is", at a "fire sale" price.

The owners of the Ronne Building accepted the buyer's offer. The building would be demolished and replaced by a multi-level parking garage for all of the nearby buildings.

Mohammed and Al Qaeda would not be mentioned anywhere in any of the events. That did not matter. Allah would be pleased that his loyal follower, Mohammed Mahmood, had been true to Islam. The Ronne Building would be gone from the Houston skyline. There had been no loss of life and no serious injuries. No one would have any idea that Al Qaeda had succeeded again. It had just not been a spectacular event, as some had come to expect from Al Qaeda. His mission completed, Mohammed informed his superiors.

Osama bin Laden again addressed President Cameron through Al Jazeera radio and by delayed tape message. "Mr. President, be careful where you stay when you are next in Houston. Our Agents have gone back to basics. Have a nice day."

www.ingramcontent.com/pod-product-compliance
Lightning Source LLC
Chambersburg PA
CBHW020312290526
45784CB00003B/1491